INVESTIGATING GHOSTS IN SCHOOLS

Matilda Snowden

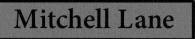

Mitchell Lane
PUBLISHERS
mitchelllane.com

2001 SW 31st Avenue
Hallandale, FL 33009

First Edition, 2021.
Author: Matilda Snowden
Designer: Ed Morgan
Editor: Joyce Markovics

Series: Investigating Ghosts!
Title: Investigating Ghosts in Schools / by Matilda Snowden

Hallandale, FL : Mitchell Lane Publishers, [2021]

Library bound ISBN: 978-1-68020-639-5
eBook ISBN: 978-1-68020-640-1

CONTENTS

Words in **bold** can be found in the Glossary.

SPOOKY SCHOOLS

A chilly wind whips up fall leaves outside an empty school. Holding a digital video recorder, a ghost hunter approaches a set of metal doors. Just then, she hears a burst of laughter coming from inside the building. She enters the school and starts filming. It's dead quiet. Broken desks, chairs, and papers litter

the floor. The silence breaks as a rat scurries across her path. Then three small figures slowly emerge from behind a desk. The ghost hunter freezes. One of the figures giggles. The others join in. All three move closer to her . . . and then vanish through a wall!

Schools are usually filled with students and teachers. It's said that some are also packed with paranormal beings. People have claimed to see and hear spooky things at schools around the country. Do spirits exist—and why do they choose to haunt certain schools? There is a devoted group who want to find out. These ghost hunters, also known as paranormal investigators, gather evidence to prove that ghosts are real.

Turn the page to read hair-raising stories about reportedly haunted schools. And follow teams of paranormal investigators who seek to uncover the truth about ghosts.

INTERESTING FACT

A recent poll found that 42 percent of Americans believe in ghosts. Ghosts are said to be the souls of dead people that appear to the living.

FARRAR SCHOOL

Maxwell, Iowa

In 2006, Jim and Nancy Oliver bought an abandoned elementary school in Iowa to use as their home. Right away, they knew there was something strange about the Farrar School. Jim and Nancy had heard stories of doors slamming and ghostly figures. But was the school really haunted?

The former Farrar School is now owned by Jim and Nancy Oliver.

One day when Nancy lost her balance on the stairs, she felt a helping hand on her shoulder. She turned around to thank Jim—only he was nowhere in sight! Another day, Nancy saw the silhouette of a boy on the stairs. "The figure stayed motionless for almost two seconds before disappearing," she said. These alarming events inspired Jim and Nancy to invite paranormal investigator Jacqui Carpenter, who's also a psychic, to check out the school in 2007.

INTERESTING FACT

The Farrar School was built in 1921 and opened in 1922. It closed in 2001.

Jacqui was thrilled to carry out an investigation because of her own spooky experience at the school. For years, she had seen a phantom girl in a window waving to her! During her investigation, Jacqui soon sensed a spirit. Using an EMF meter, Jacqui asked if the spirit was female. The meter glowed red, indicating "yes." Then she asked the spirit's age. As Jacqui counted, the red light flashed when she got to ten. Had Jacqui contacted the phantom little girl she had seen at the school?

In 2012, another investigator named Jamie Davis traveled to the Farrar School to hunt for ghosts. She brought lots of equipment, including a digital camera, an EMF meter, and flashlights. While upstairs, "I saw something out of the corner of my eye," remembers Jamie. It was a shadowy figure running. But she wasn't able to get it on film.

Paranormal investigator and psychic
Jacqui Carpenter

INTERESTING FACT

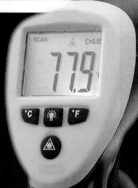

An EMF (electromagnetic field) meter is a ghost-hunting tool. Paranormal investigators believe that ghosts are made of energy. An EMF meter can help determine if a ghost is present by picking up changes in energy fields.

Jamie then used the flashlights to try to communicate with the shadow person. "If you're with us, can you turn one of those flashlights on?" she asked. All of a sudden, one of the flashlights lit up. Jamie asked the **entity** to turn the flashlight off and on again, which it did. Jamie felt chills all over. "Did I see you earlier?" she continued. The flashlight glowed, meaning "yes." Jamie felt sure she had contacted the shadow spirit she had seen earlier.

In 2016, Jim and Nancy invited a band named Ghosthive to record music at the Farrar School. On the day of the recording, engineer Griffin Landa set up a computer, headphones, and other sound equipment. Then, out of nowhere, his computer shut off. Seconds later, the screen flashed back on and the volume for the headphones was turned all the way up. "It almost blew my eardrums out," Griffin said. "I've never had stuff like that happen." After the experience, Griffin feels differently about ghosts. "I didn't necessarily believe in them until going there."

INTERESTING FACT

Paranormal investigators believe that shadow people are spirits that appear as human-shaped shadows or dark silhouettes.

CHAPTER
THREE

POCATELLO HIGH SCHOOL

Pocatello, Idaho

Many schools have school spirit—but Pocatello High School claims to have school *spirits*. In 2014, **security** cameras recorded what looks like a dark, shadowy figure in a hallway. It moved from a bench to a bathroom. The cameras also captured strange blinking lights. The **footage** drew paranormal investigator Grant Wilson and his team of ghost hunters to the Idaho school.

Pocatello High School

They first examined the security camera for anything unusual. Grant's crew soon found a large cobweb hanging off the camera. The cobweb, they decided, explained the dark figure. An important part of Grant's job is disproving claims of paranormal activity. "I don't chase ghosts," Grant said. "I chase the truth."

INTERESTING FACT

Grant and his team concluded that an electrical problem most likely caused the blinking lights.

As Grant and his team continued their investigation at Pocatello High School, they did find things they couldn't explain. Members of his team were in the auditorium when an entire row of lights dimmed. They carefully checked the room—and couldn't explain the light issue. Then some of their equipment mysteriously stopped working.

The auditorium was also where Don Cotent, former principal of Pocatello High, heard something he'll never forget. One Saturday morning, he and two advisors were working in the school when they heard the piano music coming from the auditorium. Thinking someone else was in the building, they unlocked and checked the auditorium. The room was dark and empty. Ten minutes later, the piano started playing again. "Somebody is trying to scare us," said Don. They went back to the auditorium, unlocked it, and, once again, it was empty.

INTERESTING FACT

Ghost hunters believe that ghosts can affect the energy in a room. For example, Grant has often seen equipment break down in the presence of something paranormal.

Paranormal investigator Grant Wilson

In the Pocatello High School gym, two members of Grant Wilson's team had another spooky encounter. While sitting on **bleachers**, one investigator felt a presence next to him. Then he felt something touch and then hug him. Across the gym, another investigator also felt as if she was being hugged!

"Even though a place might have [paranormal] activity, it's not bad," says Grant. Paranormal investigator Lisa Brian agrees. "Much of the paranormal is viewed as negative . . . I don't view it that way," says Lisa. She believes that spirits are drawn to places they like and want to protect, like Pocatello High School.

INTERESTING FACT

Lisa Brian is a member of SPIRO Paranormal. Started in 2008, the group investigates ghosts in and around Idaho. She has searched for ghosts at Pocatello High several times.

READFIELD SCHOOLHOUSE

Readfield, Maine

The two-story Readfield Schoolhouse in Maine was built in 1853 and once had a chapel upstairs. It remained a school for more than 130 years. Today, it's the home of the Readfield Historical Society. Because of the building's history, the first floor is set up like an old classroom. For ghost hunter Renee Alling, being in the classroom is like stepping back in time—and to an era where a phantom teacher and students might still be at work.

Readfield, Maine around 1909

Renee is the head of a group called Everything Paranormal of New England. In 2010, she and her team set up cameras and other ghost-hunting tools in the classroom. "While we're in the field, we approach the investigation with open minds," said Renee.

INTERESTING FACT

The oldest reported ghostly encounter in the country happened in Maine in 1799. People in the town of Machiasport heard knocking and a phantom woman's voice. They then saw a ghostly woman floating above the ground.

21

Renee and her team also brought several flashlights to the classroom. They asked whether a spirit in the room could light one up. Just then, one flashlight lit up. Then they asked a series of questions. Different lights flashed on and off as if responding to the questions! They believed they had contacted the spirit of a little girl. Most of the time, spirits are "trying to communicate with you," says Renee.

Later, when the team listened to the recording of the investigation, "it sounded like footsteps walking toward us," Renee said. The team also picked up the sound of a chalkboard being cleaned. Most interesting of all, they recorded what sounded like a teacher giving a grammar lesson! "This place is haunted," says Renee.

INTERESTING FACT

In 2014, investigator Tony Lewis of Zerolux Paranormal and his team visited the schoolhouse. Sensing a presence in the classroom, they asked it to make a loud noise. Suddenly, they heard three knocks. Then they heard footsteps and more knocking.

POASTTOWN ELEMENTARY SCHOOL

Middletown, Ohio

Poasttown Elementary School is located in a small, sleepy town in Ohio. But the school itself is stirring with spirits, according to Darrell Whisman who now owns the building. He wonders if past tragedies help explain why the school is haunted. In 1910, there was a train crash near where the school was built. Dozens of people died in the wreck, and victims were treated where the school now stands.

Several people died and many others were hurt during a train accident on July 4, 1910 on the Cincinnati, Hamilton, and Dayton Railroad.

Then in 1913, a flood swept through the area, killing even more people. However, Darrell strongly believes that the spirits of the dead sometimes return to the places they felt happiest. "And a lot of people were happiest in elementary school," says Darrell.

INTERESTING FACT

Poasttown Elementary School was built in 1935 and opened in 1937. Darrell Whisman attended the school when he was a child in 1963.

Darrell has invited over 100 paranormal experts to investigate Poasttown School. They've reported hearing children's footsteps and voices as well as desks moving on their own. In 2016, ghost hunter Mike Palmer and his team visited the school. He was shocked by what happened. "It's very rare for our instruments to **simultaneously** go off and do so on command," Mike said. He and his team also captured EVPs of an old man speaking. Mike is sure that something paranormal is going on at the school. Darrell says that everyone who visits the school comes away "with a new understanding of the word haunted." According to Darrell: "When you leave, you believe."

Poasttown Elementary School

INTERESTING FACT

In 2005, Mike Palmer founded a group called the Paranormal Investigators of Kentucky, or PINK. He and his team have investigated hundreds of homes, businesses, and schools throughout the country.

Ghost-Hunting Tools

Here are some basic ghost-hunting tools. Many household items can be used to track and gather evidence of possible ghosts.

- Pen and paper to record your findings
- A flashlight with extra batteries
- A camera with a clean lens (Sometimes, the "**orbs**" that some people capture on film are actually dust particles on the lens.)
- A cell phone to use in case of an emergency and to keep track of time
- A camcorder or digital video recorder to capture images of spirits or any other paranormal activity
- A digital audio recorder to capture ghostly sounds or EVPs
- A digital thermometer to pick up temperature changes

More experienced ghost hunters use **thermal** imaging tools to locate hot and cold spots, as well as special meters to pick up energy fields. These include EMF (electromagnetic field) and RF (radio frequency) meters.

FIND OUT MORE

BOOKS

Gardner Walsh, Liza. *Ghost Hunter's Handbook: Supernatural Explorations for Kids*. Lanham, Maryland: Down East Publishing, 2016.

Loh-Hagan, Virginia. *Odd Jobs: Ghost Hunter*. Ann Arbor, Michigan: Cherry Lake Publishing, 2016.

Lunis, Natalie. *Spooky Schools*. New York: Bearport Publishing, 2013.

WEBSITES

American Hauntings
https://www.americanhauntingsink.com

American Paranormal Investigations
https://www.ap-investigations.com

Ghost Research Society
http://www.ghostresearch.org

Paranormal Inc.
http://www.paranormalincorporated.com

The Parapsychological Association
https://www.parapsych.org

Zerolux Paranormal
http://www.zeroluxparanormal.com

WORKS CONSULTED

Davis, Jamie. *Haunted Asylums, Prisons, and Sanatoriums*. Woodbury, Minnesota: Llewellyn Publications, 2013.

Hawes, Jason, and Grant Wilson. *Ghost Files*. New York: Gallery Books, 2011. New York: Gallery Books, 2011.

Newman, Rich. *Ghost Hunting for Beginners: Everything You Need to Know to Get Started*. Woodbury, Minnesota: Llewellyn Publications, 2018.

Taylor, Troy. *The Ghost Hunters Guidebook: The Essential Guide to Investigating Ghosts & Hauntings*. Alton, Illinois: Whitechapel Productions Press, 2004.

Verde, Thomas. *Maine Ghosts & Legends: 28 Encounters with the Supernatural*. Camden, Maine: Down East Books, 2013.

ON THE INTERNET

https://fringeparanormal.wordpress.com/2013/10/07/the-paranormal-at-home-hauntings-in-50-states-iowas-farrar-schoolhouse/

http://www.ghostresearch.org/Investigations/farrar.html

http://www.ghosttheory.com/2010/06/01/haunted-schoolhouse-team-finds-paranormal-activity

https://hauntingatfarrar.com

https://www.idahostatejournal.com/news/local/new-ghost-hunters-show-will-apparently-feature-haunted-pocatello-high/article_0e9b8b5e-7aa6-534b-a942-32e15ffcd31f.html

https://www.poasttownschool.com/history

https://www.wcpo.com/longform/inside-poasttown-elementary-butler-countys-haunted-abandoned-school

GLOSSARY

abandoned
No longer lived in

auditorium
A theater with seating for many people

bleachers
A set of benches arranged like steps for people to sit on while they are watching a sporting event or performance

devoted
Very loyal

electromagnetic field
A field of energy around a magnetic material or moving electric charge

emerge
To come into view

engineer
A person who works with machines

entity
A distinct being

evidence
Information and facts that help prove something

footage
Film that has not been edited

orbs
Glowing spheres

paranormal
Relating to events not able to be scientifically explained

phantom
A ghost or spirit

presence
The state of being present in a place

psychic
A person claiming to have powers not able to be scientifically explained

security
Relating to things that help keep people safe

silhouette
The dark shape and outline of someone or something

simultaneously
At the same time

spirits
Supernatural beings such as ghosts

thermal
Relating to heat

tragedies
Events that cause great suffering

vanish
To disappear

Index

About the Author

Matilda Snowden loves all things old and cobwebby. Her favorite thing about being an author is visiting schools, sharing her love of books, and talking with children about how to tell a spooky story.